THE PARK

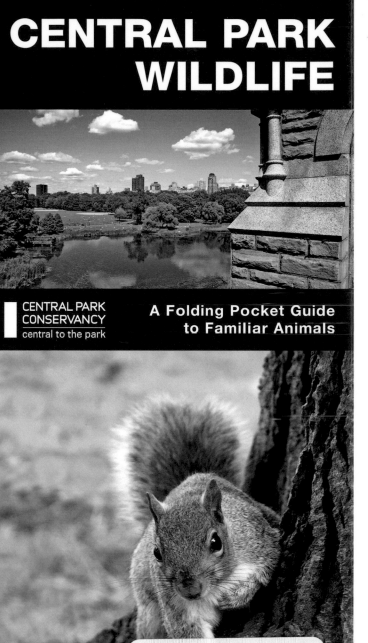

1. Harlem Meer
   Best Fishing
2. Charles A. Dana Discovery Center
3. The Pool
4. Jacqueline Kennedy Onassis Reservoir
5. Arthur Ross Pinetum
6. Turtle Pond
7. The Lake
8. The Ramble
   Best Birding
9. The Point
10. Central Park Zoo
11. Hallett Nature Sanctuary
12. The Pond

New York City's Central Park is an 843-acre urban oasis that provides a habitat for many species of plants and animals. With 20,000 trees and several bodies of water, the Park is a magnet for more than 280 species of birds. For more information about tours, education, and community programs, visit centralparknyc.org.

CENTRAL PARK CONSERVANCY
central to the park

Waterford Press produces reference guides that introduce novices to nature, science, travel and languages. Product information is featured on the website:
www.waterfordpress.com

Text and illustrations © 2012, 2017 by Waterford Press Inc. All rights reserved.
Cover images © iStock Photo.
For permissions, call 800-434-2555.
To order, call 800-434-2555.

For permissions, or to share comments, e-mail editor@waterfordpress.com.
For information on custom-published products, call 800-2555 or e-mail info@waterfordpress.com.

ISBN 978-1-58355-774-7 $7.95 U.S.

Made in the USA

710401

CENTRAL PARK WILDLIFE

CENTRAL PARK CONSERVANCY
central to the park

A Folding Pocket Guide to Familiar Animals

CENTRAL PARK WILDLIFE – A Folding Pocket Guide to Familiar Animals   Kavanagh/Leung

---

POND INVERTEBRATES

 Water Boatman
Family Corixidae
I o .5 in. (1.3 cm)
An erratic swimmer with oar-like limbs. Often clings to submerged plants.

 **Backswimmer**
Family Notonectidae
To .5 in. (1.3 cm)
Swims on its back. Often rests at or just below the surface.

Pond Leech
Macrobdella spp.
To 10 in. (25 cm)
Red or black spots mark the sides.

Water Flea
Daphnia pulex
To .02 in. (.5 mm)

Whirligig Beetle
Family Gyrinidae
To .5 in. (1.3 cm)
Oval insect swims in circles on the water's surface.

 Mosquito
Family Culicidae
To .5 in. (1.3 cm)
Slender insect has a thin, blood-sucking beak.

Mosquito larvae are found floating at the water's surface

Giant Pond Snail
Lymnaea stagnalis
To 2.5 in. (6 cm)

Water Strider
Gerris spp. To .5 in. (1.3 cm)
Long-legged insect skates along the surface of the water without breaking through.

 **Pond Crayfish**
Procambarus spp.
To 5 in. (13 cm)

Mayfly
Order Ephemeroptera
To 1.25 in. (3.2 cm)
Has triangular wings and long 'tails'.

Water Scorpion
Family Nepidae
To 1.75 in. (4.5 cm)
Stick-like bug has claw-like front legs.

 **Stonefly**
Order Plecoptera
To 2.5 in. (6 cm)
Blackish adult has wings folded flat over its abdomen.

Caddisfly
Order Trichoptera
To 1 in. (3 cm)
Has hairy wings and long antennae.

Black-winged Damselfly
Calopteryx maculata
To 1.75 in. (4.5 cm)
Like all damselflies, it rests with its wings held together over its back.

Green Darner
Anax junius
To 3 in. (8 cm)
Has blue-to-green thorax. A dragonfly, it rests with its wings open.

BUTTERFLIES

Black Swallowtail
Papilio polyxenes
To 3.5 in. (9 cm)
Black, yellow and blue butterfly has two rows of yellow spots on its forewing.

Eastern Tiger Swallowtail
Papilio glaucus
To 6 in. (15 cm)

Spicebush Swallowtail
Papilio troilus
To 4.5 in. (11 cm)
Also called the green-clouded swallowtail for its greenish hindwings.

Orange Sulphur
Colias eurytheme
To 2.5 in. (6 cm)

Eastern Tailed Blue
Everes comyntas
To 1 in. (3 cm)

Banded Hairstreak
Satyrium calanus
To 1.25 in. (3.2 cm)

 Pearl Crescent
Phyciodes tharos
To 1.5 in. (4 cm)

Comma
Polygonia comma
To 2 in. (5 cm)

Zabulon Skipper
Poanes zabulon
To 1.5 in. (4 cm)

Question Mark
Polygonia interrogationis
To 2.5 in. (6 cm)
Note ragged wing margins. Silvery mark on underwings resembles a question mark or semi-colon.

Cabbage Butterfly
Pieris rapae
To 2 in. (5 cm)
Whitish butterfly has dark wing spots.

Silver-spotted Skipper
Epargyreus clarus
To 2.5 in. (6 cm)
Has a large irregular silver patch on the underside of its hindwing.

Underside shown

Red Admiral
Vanessa atalanta
To 2.5 in. (6 cm)
Males defend territories vigorously and often divebomb passing insects and even people.

Mourning Cloak
Nymphalis antiopa
To 4 in. (10 cm)

Monarch Caterpillar

Mourning Cloak

Monarch
Danaus plexippus
To 4 in. (10 cm)
Note rows of white spots on edges of wings. Annual migration may cover thousands of miles.

Tiger Swallowtail

FRESHWATER FISHES

Largemouth Bass
Micropterus salmoides To 40 in. (1 m)
Jaw joint extends beyond the eye.

Pumpkinseed
Lepomis gibbosus
To 16 in. (40 cm)

Common Carp
Cyprinus carpio To 30 in. (75 cm)
Has 2 mouth barbels and a forked, orangish tail.

Bluegill
Lepomis macrochirus
To 16 in. (40 cm)

Golden Shiner
Notemigonus crysoleucas
To 12 in. (30 cm)

Catfish
Ictalurus spp. To 4 ft. (1.2 m)
Chubby fish has prominent mouth barbels (whiskers).

Brown Bullhead
Ameiurus nebulosus
To 20 in. (50 cm)

Fathead Minnow
Pimephales promelas To 4 in. (10 cm)
Breeding male has a 'bumpy' head.

Goldfish
Carassius auratus To 16 in. (40 cm)
Color ranges from gold to white.

Yellow Perch
Perca flavescens To 16 in. (40 cm)
Has 6-9 dark 'saddles' down side.

Shiner
Notropis spp. To 5 in. (13 cm)
Note that dorsal fin originates behind the pelvic fin.

Banded Killifish
Fundulus diaphanus
To 5 in. (13 cm)

REPTILES & AMPHIBIANS

Snapping Turtle
Chelydra serpentina To 18 in. (45 cm)
Note large head, knobby shell and long tail.

Painted Turtle
Chrysemys picta To 10 in. (25 cm)
Note red marks on outer edge of shell.

Pond Slider
Trachemys scripta To 11 in. (28 cm)
Has yellow, red or orange stripe on head.

Cooter
Pseudemys concinna To 16 in. (40 cm)
Note prominent neck markings.

Tadpole

Green Frog
Lithobates clamitans To 4 in. (10 cm)
Single-note call is a banjo-like twang.

Tadpole

Bullfrog
Lithobates catesbeianus
To 8 in. (20 cm)
Call is a deep-pitched – *jug-o-rum*.

MAMMALS

 **Common Raccoon**
Procyon lotor
To 40 in. (1 m)

Eastern Chipmunk
Tamias striatus
To 12 in. (30 cm)

Eastern Red Bat
Lasiurus borealis
To 5 in. (13 cm)

Eastern Cottontail
Sylvilagus floridanus
To 18 in. (45 cm)

Eastern Gray Squirrel
Sciurus carolinensis
To 20 in. (50 cm)

Groundhog
Marmota monax
To 32 in. (80 cm)

Deer Mouse
Peromyscus maniculatus
To 8 in. (20 cm)
Has white undersides and a hairy tail.

Common Loon
Gavia immer To 3 ft. (90 cm)
Winter
Summer

Pied-billed Grebe
Podilymbus podiceps
To 13 in. (33 cm)

Mute Swan
Cygnus olor
To 5 ft. (1.5 m)
Orange bill has a black knob at the base.

Canada Goose
Branta canadensis
To 43 in. (1.1 m)

Mallard
Anas platyrhynchos To 28 in. (70 cm)

American Black Duck
Anas rubripes
To 25 in. (63 cm)

Gadwall
Anas strepera To 23 in. (58 cm)

Wood Duck
Aix sponsa To 20 in. (50 cm)

Green-winged Teal
Anas crecca To 16 in. (40 cm)

Lesser Scaup
Aythya affinis To 18 in. (45 cm)

Northern Shoveler
Anas clypeata To 20 in. (50 cm)
Named for its large spatulate bill.

Canvasback
Aythya valisineria To 2 ft. (60 cm)
Note sloping forehead.

Bufflehead
Bucephala albeola
To 15 in. (38 cm)

Ruddy Duck
Oxyura jamaicensis
To 16 in. (40 cm)

Common Merganser
Mergus merganser To 27 in. (68 cm)

American Coot
Fulica americana
To 16 in. (40 cm)

Great Egret
Ardea alba
To 38 in. (95 cm)
Note yellow bill and black feet.

Great Blue Heron
Ardea herodias
To 4.5 ft. (1.4 m)

Green Heron
Butorides virescens
To 22 in. (55 cm)

Black-crowned Night-Heron
Nycticorax nycticorax
To 28 in. (70 cm)

Double-crested Cormorant
Phalacrocorax auritus
To 3 ft. (90 cm)

Snowy Egret
Egretta thula
To 26 in. (65 cm)
Note black bill and yellow feet.

Ring-billed Gull
Larus delawarensis
To 20 in. (50 cm)
Bill has dark ring.

Herring Gull
Larus smithsonianus
To 26 in. (65 cm)
Wing tips are black with white spots.
Legs are pinkish.

Great Black-backed Gull
Larus marinus
To 32 in. (80 cm)
Note large size.

Common Tern
Sterna hirundo
To 15 in. (38 cm)

Chimney Swift
Chaetura pelagica
To 6 in. (15 cm)

Great Horned Owl
Bubo virginianus
To 25 in. (63 cm)
Call is a resonant – hoo-HOO-hoooo.

Cooper's Hawk
Accipiter cooperii
To 20 in. (50 cm)
Note long, rounded white-tipped tail.

Red-tailed Hawk
Buteo jamaicensis
To 25 in. (63 cm)

Sharp-shinned Hawk
Accipiter striatus
To 14 in. (35 cm)
Note long, square-edged tail and striped breast.

American Kestrel
Falco sparverius
To 12 in. (30 cm)

Wild Turkey
Meleagris gallopavo
To 4 ft. (1.2 m)

Mourning Dove
Zenaida macroura
To 13 in. (33 cm)

Belted Kingfisher
Megaceryle alcyon
To 14 in. (35 cm)

Ruby-throated Hummingbird
Archilochus colubris
To 3.5 in. (9 cm)

Rock Pigeon
Columba livia
To 13 in. (33 cm)

Northern Flicker
Colaptes auratus
To 13 in. (33 cm)
Wing and tail linings are yellow.

Red-bellied Woodpecker
Melanerpes carolinus
To 11 in. (28 cm)

Downy Woodpecker
Picoides pubescens
To 6 in. (15 cm)
The similar hairy woodpecker is larger and has a longer bill.

Eastern Kingbird
Tyrannus tyrannus
To 8 in. (20 cm)

Great Crested Flycatcher
Myiarchus crinitus
To 8 in. (20 cm)

Eastern Phoebe
Sayornis phoebe
To 7 in. (18 cm)

Barn Swallow
Hirundo rustica
To 8 in. (20 cm)
Note deeply forked tail.

Tufted Titmouse
Baeolophus bicolor
To 6 in. (15 cm)

Black-capped Chickadee
Poecile atricapillus
To 6 in. (15 cm)

Northern Rough-winged Swallow
Stelgidopteryx serripennis
To 6 in. (15 cm)
Note dusky throat.

Red-eyed Vireo
Vireo olivaceus
To 6 in. (15 cm)

Golden-crowned Kinglet
Regulus satrapa
To 3.5 in. (9 cm)

White-breasted Nuthatch
Sitta carolinensis
To 6 in. (15 cm)

Winter Wren
Troglodytes troglodytes
To 4 in. (10 cm)

House Wren
Troglodytes aedon
To 5 in. (13 cm)

Blue Jay
Cyanocitta cristata
To 14 in. (35 cm)

European Starling
Sturnus vulgaris
To 8 in. (20 cm)

American Crow
Corvus brachyrhynchos
To 22 in. (55 cm)
Call is a distinct – caw.

Brown-headed Cowbird
Molothrus ater
To 7 in. (18 cm)

Red-winged Blackbird
Agelaius phoeniceus
To 9 in. (23 cm)

Common Grackle
Quiscalus quiscula
To 14 in. (35 cm)

American Robin
Turdus migratorius
To 11 in. (28 cm)

Hermit Thrush
Catharus guttatus
To 7 in. (18 cm)
Note rusty tail and spotted breast.

Swainson's Thrush
Catharus ustulatus
To 7 in. (18 cm)

Cedar Waxwing
Bombycilla cedrorum
To 7 in. (18 cm)
Red wing marks look like waxy droplets.

Northern Mockingbird
Mimus polyglottos
To 11 in. (28 cm)

Gray Catbird
Dumetella carolinensis
To 9 in. (23 cm)
Note black cap and reddish undertail feathers.

Yellow Warbler
Setophaga petechia
To 5 in. (13 cm)

'Myrtle' Race

Northern Parula
Setophaga americana
To 4.5 in. (11 cm)

American Redstart
Setophaga ruticilla
To 5 in. (13 cm)

Yellow-rumped Warbler
Setophaga coronata
To 6 in. (15 cm)
Note yellow on rump and crown and white throat.

Black-and-white Warbler
Mniotilta varia
To 6 in. (15 cm)

Common Yellowthroat
Geothlypis trichas
To 5 in. (13 cm)

Black-throated Blue Warbler
Setophaga caerulescens
To 6 in. (15 cm)

Chestnut-sided Warbler
Setophaga pensylvanica
To 6 in. (15 cm)
Note chestnut sides and yellow crown.

Ovenbird
Seiurus aurocapilla
To 6 in. (15 cm)
Distinctive call is – tea-cher, tea-cher.

Blackburnian Warbler
Setophaga fusca
To 5 in. (13 cm)
Note orange throat.

Palm Warbler
Setophaga palmarum
To 6 in. (15 cm)

Northern Waterthrush
Parkesia noveboracensis
To 6 in. (15 cm)
Found near water, it teeters while walking.

Canada Warbler
Cardellina canadensis
To 6 in. (15 cm)
Note black 'necklace'.

White-throated Sparrow
Zonotrichia albicollis
To 7 in. (18 cm)
Note white throat and yellow spot in front of eye.

Baltimore Oriole
Icterus galbula
To 8 in. (20 cm)
Black and orange bird has a full black cap.

Song Sparrow
Melospiza melodia
To 7 in. (18 cm)
Note central breast spot.

Chipping Sparrow
Spizella passerina
To 6 in. (15 cm)
Note chestnut cap.

House Sparrow
Passer domesticus
To 6 in. (15 cm)

Eastern Towhee
Pipilo erythrophthalmus
To 9 in. (23 cm)

'Slate-colored' Race

Dark-eyed Junco
Junco hyemalis
To 7 in. (18 cm)

Scarlet Tanager
Piranga olivacea
To 7 in. (18 cm)

American Goldfinch
Spinus tristis
To 5 in. (13 cm)

House Finch
Haemorhous mexicanus
To 6 in. (15 cm)

Northern Cardinal
Cardinalis cardinalis
To 9 in. (23 cm)